# LEARNING TO SWIM
## is fun
## on holidays in the sun

Maeve Grimes

illustrated by
Mariia Furdei

Great Adventure Street

Platform 4

11:30

Holidays come once a year,
We are so excited to pack
Our swimming gear.

Our journey begins
By boarding the train,
We are heading to the sun
Away from the rain.

Sarah has done great for today.
Look what she has done all through play

Walk along slowly,
No need to burst

An adult must always
Get in the pool first

Take a deep breath in
And hold it for ten,
Remember to practice
Again and again

# Mummy reminds us along the way,
# The lessons we learned on our last holiday.

Walk along slowly
No need to burst,

An adult must always
Get in the pool first.

Take a deep breath in
And hold it for ten,
Practise this again and again.

A cabin in the woods filled with fun things to do,
A pool table, bunk beds even a Jacuzzi too.

So many adventures with swimming pools
and slides,

Rollercoasters, zip wires and carnival rides

The waterpark is the first place we go,
Into the baby pool but remember go slow,

All the girls sit down on the step,
We start with our kicking taking in a deep
breath.

Daddy minds the baby,
It's his first time in the pool,
He cradles him into a float,
Supporting his head is the most important
rule.

Blowing out bubbles in the water while we kick,
Our bubbles go slow and our legs go quick.

Let's practise this now by having a race,
Crawl like crocodiles,
Kick our legs with pace.

Sarah was the first to get to the other side, Daddy says, 'two more games before we go to the carnival ride'.

Mummy is in the middle, we sit on the side,
This is a great way to practise our glide.

Arms out straight in front, head goes in the water,
Abby pushes from the step this is what Mummy taught her.

'Right', said Mummy. 'Get back to the side'
'Push off me and practise your glide'.

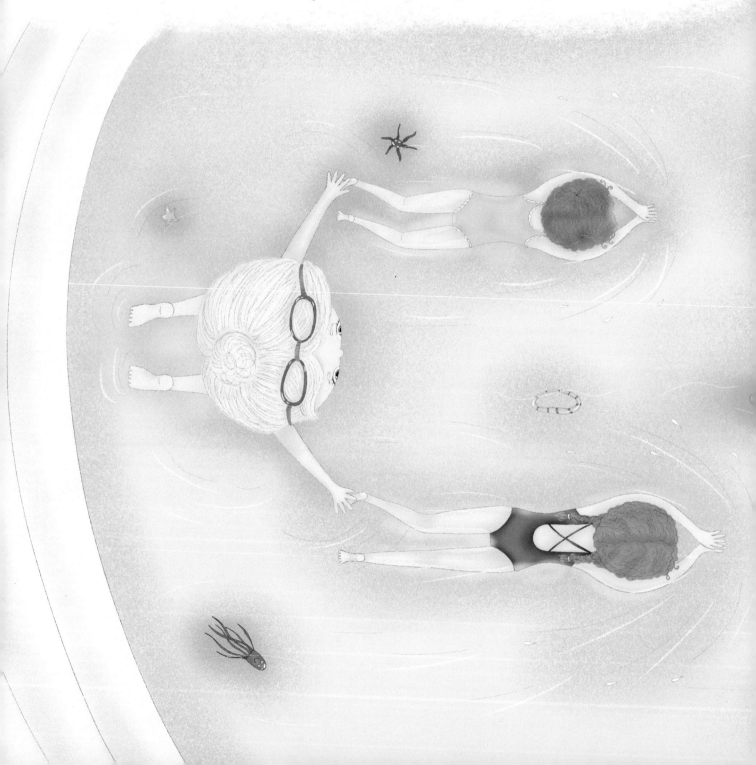

Next we glide in the shape of an arrow,
Point our toes, arms cover our ears and
our hands go narrow.

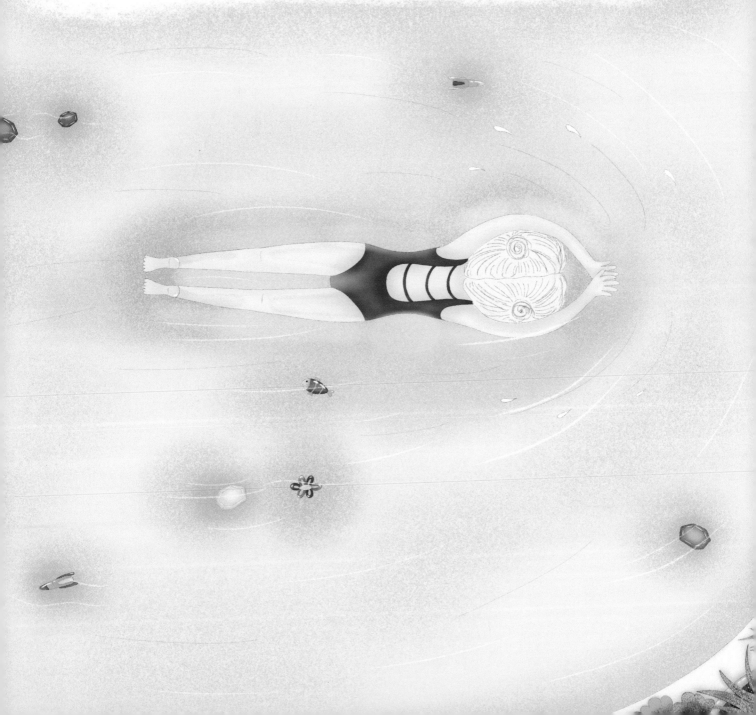

With curled up bunny legs,
You start at the wall,
'Push off hard', Mummy says.
'And stretch yourself tall'.

When our glide slows,
We add in a kick using our pointy toes.
We are superheroes travelling really fast,
Mummy cheers us on as we all go passed.

Learning to float is fun,
On holidays in the Sun.
Look at us in the pool,
Floating is really cool.

Lie back pretend you are in bed,
Belly up and relax your head.
Mummy holds your
shoulders,
It will settle you
to start.

She will help you
roll over,
You are mastering
the art.

If you ever get tired and need a rest,
Turn on your back and relax is BEST,

If you ever get out of your depth and can't swim,
Turn on your back, relax and you will be safe again.

We haven't much time left,
So we go to the slides.
We all choose the twisty one
'HURRAY', we all cry.

We get to the changing room,
With no time to lose.
Our next adventure is around the corner,
So many rides to choose.

Candy floss, popcorn and hotdogs to smell,
Bumper cars, swings and galloping
carousel.

We finish the day with a roller coaster ride,
'Let's do it all again tomorrow', Daddy cried.

Follow us on our next amazing adventure where we will fly somewhere very special. Swimming Strokes for Young Folks will give you a step by step guide to complete your stroke and progress you to swimming lengths. Together we will master the skill of frontstroke and backstroke while inspiring your Littleswimmerz to dream big!

# SWIMMING STROKES

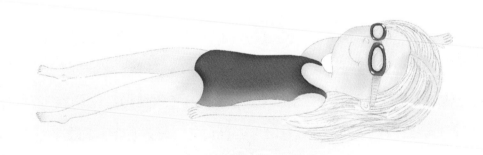

# FOR YOUNG FOLKS

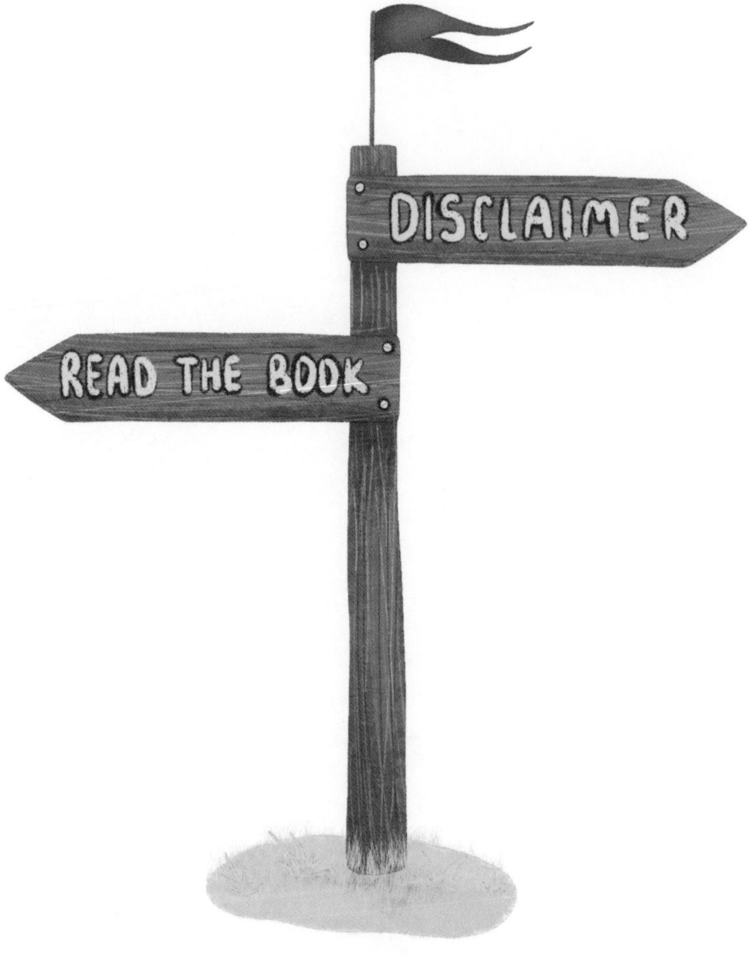
DISCLAIMER
READ THE BOOK

Printed in Poland
by Amazon Fulfillment
Poland Sp. z o.o., Wrocław